A Kid's Guide to

GENEALOGY

Clifton Park - Halfmoon Public Library
475 Moe Road
Clifton Park, New York 12065

HOW TO
RESEARCH YOUR
ANCESTRY

Tamra Orr

Mitchell Lane
PUBLISHERS
P.O. Box 196
Hockessin, Delaware 19707

Mitchell Lane

PUBLISHERS

Basic Genealogy for Kids
How to Research Your Ancestry
Using Technology to Find Your Family History
Design Your Family Tree

Printing   1   2   3   4   5   6   7   8   9

**Library of Congress
Cataloging-in-Publication Data**
Orr, Tamra.
  How to research your ancestry / by Tamra Orr.
      p. cm.—(A kid's guide to genealogy)
  Includes bibliographical references and index.
  ISBN 978-1-58415-950-6 (library bound)
  1. Genealogy—Juvenile literature. I. Title.
  CS15.5.O77 2011
  929'.1072—dc22

                                                    2011002754

eBook ISBN: 9781612280936

PLB

4838

Contents

Introduction 4

Chapter One
   Planting a Family Tree 7

Chapter Two
   Digging for Your Roots 13

Chapter Three
   Branching Out 21

Chapter Four
   Growing a Family Tree 31

Chapter Five
   Sending Out Shoots 39

Further Reading 44

   Books 44

   Works Consulted 44

   On the Internet 45

Glossary 46

Index 47

Words in **bold** type can be found in the glossary.

INTRODUCTION

Even though it has been almost forty years, I can still remember a particular day in class at elementary school. My teacher was talking about how to trace our ancestry, and I wanted to add something. I raised my hand.

"My family goes back a long way. My grandpa told me that I'm related to President George Washington's wife, Martha," I said proudly.

Instead of amazed *oohs* and *aahs*, however, I only saw frowns and looks of disbelief.

"Really!" I added. It didn't seem to help.

That night I went home and called my grandfather, who had spent years tracing our family history. He told me I was right. I *was* a very distant relative of Martha Washington. Grandpa loaned me the book that showed the generations, and I took it to school with me. The same grin spreads across my face today as I recall the grudging looks of acceptance from my classmates. At that moment, I knew that finding out about my ancestors was important. I've been interested ever since.

In a way, your family is like a series of branches from a tree that has kept growing through generations.

CHAPTER 1:
PLANTING A
FAMILY TREE

Have you ever looked at a big tree growing in a backyard or in a city park? Did you look at the thick trunk with its brown bark? Did you look up and try to count the branches covered in leaves? Did you ever wonder about the tiny seed that started that huge tree? Have you thought about where that seed came from—and the seed before it? How about the seed before that one? Where might it have been before it fell to the ground? Did the breeze blow it there, or did it arrive some other way?

That curiosity is the same one that inspires many people to start looking for where they came from—and the generation before them and the one before that one. Studying the family that came before you is known as **genealogy,** and it can be fascinating!

Everyone has different reasons for wanting to trace his or her family history. Some might be looking for a long-lost relative. Some might be curious about what part of the country they came from. Some might want to see where their families were at important points in history.

But then, some might just be trying to get a Boy Scout merit badge.

Master Termite's Family
Andrew Hobson wanted to earn his Boy Scout Genealogy Merit Badge. To help him with the project,

Like these soldiers, Uncle John Parsons was a paratrooper who fought in Europe during World War II.

his parents sat down and the entire family looked through photographs, letters, newspaper clippings, and other old family papers. Both Andrew and his brother Ian loved looking through the World War II paratrooper photos of their great-great uncle John Parsons. Uncle John had been with the 504th Parachute Infantry of the 82nd Airborne Division, and the family had a number of stories about him. Ian had a question, though: Where was Uncle John buried?

A little research help from their parents turned up military grave records, and from those they could locate a cemetery. One question was answered—but in the process, a bigger one came up. During the online research, Mrs. Hobson noticed that the name John Parsons had an unusual number of hits. A book title kept popping up. Parsons' name appeared in multiple military discussion forums. Even a new nickname was mentioned over and over:

S/Sgt Ross S. Carter

Master Termite. The Hobsons grew more and more curious.

What the Hobsons discovered was that their favorite great-great uncle John was also many people's favorite. His adventures and bravery in the war had been included in a popular biography published in 1951. Called *Those Devils in Baggy Pants,* it was written by Ross Carter, one of the only three soldiers in the platoon to have survived the war. In it, Parsons was nicknamed Master Termite. The family was thrilled to find out that their relative was a legend!

The family's adventure in tracing their ancestry was not quite over, though. The Hobsons noticed that the people on these forums were disappointed there weren't any photographs of Parsons to be found. A historian left an e-mail address on his site in hopes of one day hearing from Master Termite's family. The message was old, but the Hobsons took a chance and e-mailed anyway. They heard

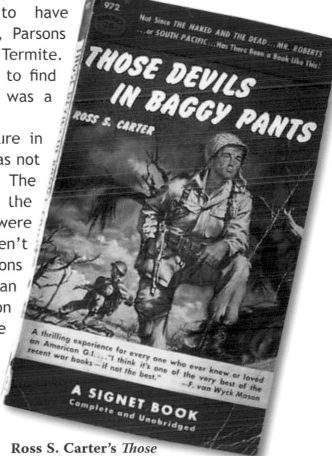

Ross S. Carter's *Those Devils in Baggy Pants*

back right away. Soon, the Hobsons were sharing photos and stories online with historical groups and historians from all over the world. Discovering Master Termite proved to be a real adventure in genealogy.

Oh, and yes. Andrew did indeed get his Boy Scout merit badge.

Your Personal Puzzle

Tracing your history and learning about the family that came before you may not always turn up someone famous, but it will teach you all about where you came from and everyone who helped make you exactly who you are today. Some people compare the search to putting together a puzzle. One woman, 82, had been researching her family history for years. She said, "Genealogy is such a fascinating puzzle and it is one that never ends. As soon as

Start collecting clues to the past like pieces of a puzzle.

you find one answer, it only brings up more questions. For a person who likes puzzles, there is nothing better."

If you are ready, you can put together your puzzle by exploring your family tree, seeing who makes up each of its branches and finding out precisely where those first seeds came from.

Before you start tracing your ancestors, select a special notebook for all the papers and notes you will collect. It should include multiple folders to hold the forms and other sheets of paper you will gather in your search. You can decorate your notebook with whatever you want. Use stickers and glitter. Illustrate the cover with your drawings or copies of photographs. Your notebook is the roadmap for your genealogy journey.

Look at yourself carefully and decide what things make you exactly you.

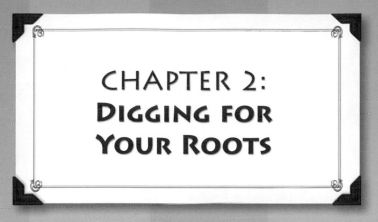

CHAPTER 2:
DIGGING FOR YOUR ROOTS

What is the first step in exploring your family tree? It's an easy one. Just find the closest mirror and take a look in it. That's right! The first step in genealogy is finding out more about yourself. That is simple, too. Just ask yourself questions and write down the answers in your notebook.

To write "The Story of Me," begin by writing down all the details you know about yourself. You may be shocked at how much information you already know.

The basic facts to include are:

- Your full name (first, middle, and last)
- Any nicknames and the story behind them
- Who you were named after/the history of your name
- The day, month, and year you were born
- The city, state, and country in which you were born

Once you've done that, you can step back one more generation to your parents. Try to find a time to sit down with your mother and father and ask them some of the same questions. Be sure to write down the answers. You may think you will remember all of it—but as you gather more and more information, you may forget important details if they are not written down.

- Your mother's full name, including her **maiden name**
- Your mother's date of birth
- Your mother's place of birth
- Your father's full name
- Your father's date of birth
- Your father's place of birth
- The date your parents were married
- The place your parents were married
- The same information for any stepparents
- Full names of aunts and uncles
- Birth dates and birthplaces of aunts and uncles

What if your parents are divorced? You can record the official divorce date. Make sure you write down all the details if either of your parents gets married again. Then you can add the following information:

- The full names of any of your siblings
- The birth dates and birthplaces of any siblings or step or half siblings
- The street address, city, state, and zip code of where you currently live
- The street address, city, state and zip code of other places you have lived
- If you were adopted, add when and where you were adopted, plus any other details you might have

Now you've covered the basics of your generation and the next one (your parents). Take it one step further and find out the same details from your **maternal** and **paternal** grandparents. Include their full names, including maiden names; birthdays and places of birth (and death, if that applies); and their dates and places of marriages.

A family's four generations of women pose for a picture.

With that information, you have a great start. In just a short time, you have gathered basic information on three generations: you and your brothers and sisters, your parents and their brothers and sisters, and both sets of grandparents. Besides writing it down in your notebook, you have enough data to create a basic family tree. Genealogy trees come in different designs, and many free examples can be found online. Here are a few examples:

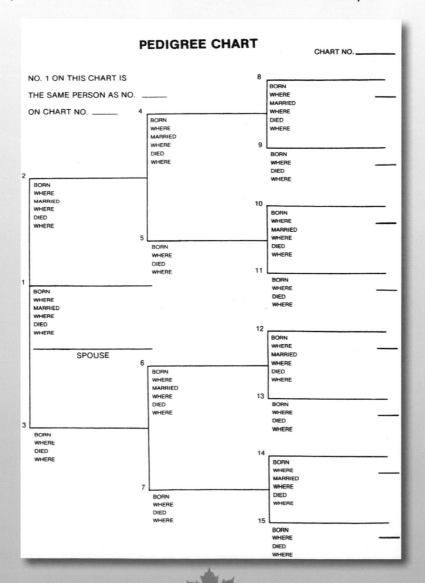

My Family Tree

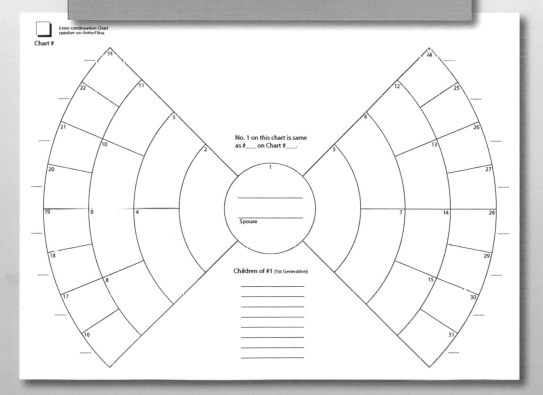

23

22   11

21   5

10   2

20   1

No. 1 on this chart is same
as # ____ on Chart # ____.

_____
_____
Spouse

19   9   4   7   14   28

18   27

17   8   15   30

16   31

24

25

12

6   26

3   13

Children of #1 (1st Generation)

_____
_____
_____
_____
_____
_____

If you don't like what you find online, feel free to create your own in whatever style and shape you like the best. Just because it is called a family tree does not mean you have to use that shape. Let your imagination decide how it should look.

Other Resources in the House

Getting the information about your parents and grandparents may be as simple as sitting down to talk to them. However, often it is a bit more complicated. Perhaps they are busy or live far away. There are many ways to work around this problem, and we will examine those in the next chapter. First, however, let's look at other resources you can use to find some of this important information.

Take a look at this list. How many of these items do you think you have around the house? If you aren't sure, ask your parents. They might point you to a box in the attic or a stash in a cupboard. Each of these items holds many important keys and details to your family history:

- Diaries or journals, calendars, and date books
- Family Bible
- Wedding, birth, and funeral announcements
- Photos and photo albums, slides, or CDs of photographs
- Diplomas, certificates, and awards
- Newspaper clippings
- Yearbooks and other school papers
- Letters and postcards
- Scrapbooks

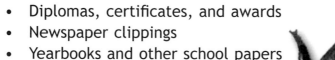

Each of these resources can help you gather the dates and facts you need. But they can do much more than that. Photos and slides can put actual faces to names. Backgrounds, furniture, clothing, and scenery can help you better understand the time period of your relatives. Journals, date books, and diaries can introduce you to them in a very personal way as you read their thoughts and opinions. Letters can show you what their daily lives were like. Exploring these resources and learning from them is part of genealogy and the ongoing search for meeting your ancestors.

Of course, genealogy is much more than names, dates, and places. There is much more to find out when you study your ancestors. You can learn a great deal from the resources listed here, but the best way to get essential details is through asking questions. You can do this in person, over the phone, and through e-mails and letters. Knowing what questions to ask and how to record the answers is important, so let's explore that topic next.

Does your family have its own **crest?** Many families do. You can find out if your family has one by checking out sites such as Family Crests and House of Names. If you cannot find one, why not create your own? What should go in it? What symbols are important to your family? You can use these ideas to design a crest. Find out more about how to do it online at sites such as Make Your Coat of Arms or How to Design Your Own Family Crest.

You can start your research by asking your grandparents what they remember about their relatives.

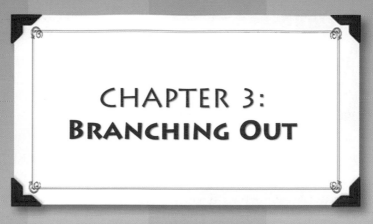

CHAPTER 3:
BRANCHING OUT

You've learned quite a bit about yourself, your parents, and your siblings. You know birth dates and marriage dates. You know where three generations were born. But there is much more to tracing your ancestry than numbers and locations. There are important stories of how couples first met each other, where they worked, what traveling they did, and how and why they became who they were. To find that out, you will need to do some in-depth detective work.

A great place to start is with **interviews,** where you can help people recall memories as well as important family stories. Interviews create "oral histories"—stories told out loud. You may be shy about interviewing people, but it's as simple as just talking to people and listening to what they say. First, let's find out the different ways you can conduct an interview. Then we will explore how to make an interview not only much easier, but also more effective.

Getting in Contact
There are a number of ways you can contact the people you want to talk to. Each method has its advantages and disadvantages. Ask the people if they would like to be interviewed, and whether they would prefer one method to another. If you are using any

method besides letters or e-mails, set up a date and time for the interview, so that both of you can give your full attention to the conversation. Ask them to bring a few photos if they have them. Be sure to take notes, and record the conversation, if possible, so that you can listen to it again. Include the date, time, and location of the interview, as well as the names of whoever is present. If you have any questions later, you can go back and check your notes or your recordings.

Face to face. Sitting down to talk to relatives in person is often the best way to do an interview. You can not only hear their words but also their tone of voice. You can see the looks on their

Start your interviews with your parents. Get them talking and you'll discover a lot about your relatives, from aunts and uncles to lots of cousins.

faces and how they move their hands, arms, and bodies. All of this can help you better understand what they are telling you. Are they excited or saddened by the memory? Is the story full of sharp details or is it hard for them to remember clearly?

If you are interviewing your close family members, you may be able to do it face to face because they either live with you or nearby. You might even schedule a special visit if your relatives live within a few hours of your house.

A great time to conduct interviews is during family gatherings, such as weddings or reunions. Ask your parents to bring a video recorder, and you can record your interviews as well as the family festivities. These interviews may not be as formal as other ones, but people tend to remember a lot of fun family stories at these cheerful events.

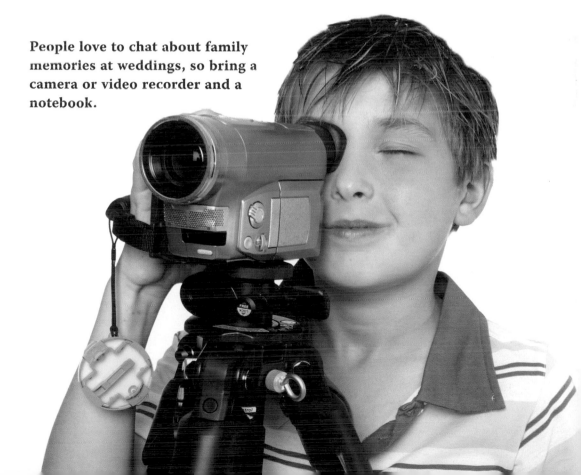

People love to chat about family memories at weddings, so bring a camera or video recorder and a notebook.

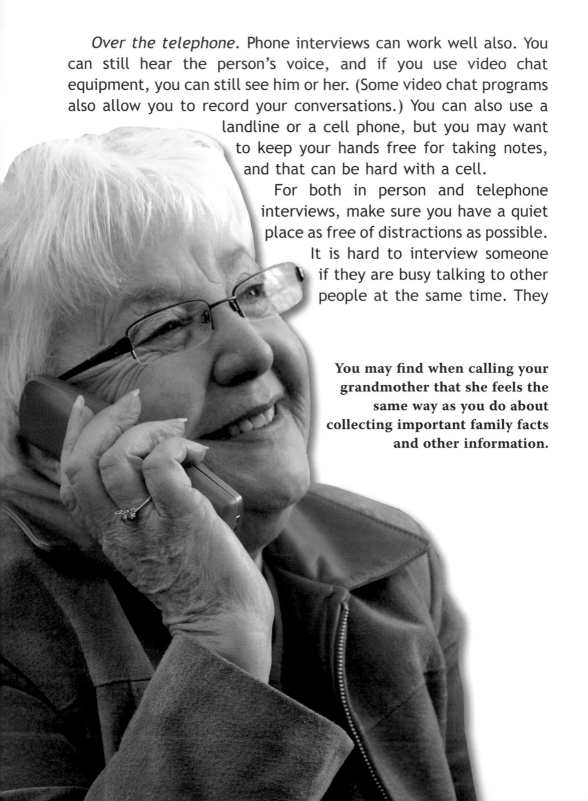

Over the telephone. Phone interviews can work well also. You can still hear the person's voice, and if you use video chat equipment, you can still see him or her. (Some video chat programs also allow you to record your conversations.) You can also use a landline or a cell phone, but you may want to keep your hands free for taking notes, and that can be hard with a cell.

For both in person and telephone interviews, make sure you have a quiet place as free of distractions as possible. It is hard to interview someone if they are busy talking to other people at the same time. They

You may find when calling your grandmother that she feels the same way as you do about collecting important family facts and other information.

You will be amazed as the story of your family grows if you get Mom talking.

will have trouble giving you the focus and attention your questions need to be fully answered. The same is true for you! Make sure you are not listening to other people around you when you do your interview.

On the computer. If you have a computer but don't have the ability to video chat, you can still do an interview through instant messaging (IM), e-mailing, or using a social network such as Facebook. The biggest advantage with IM is that it is immediate and, since the response is in writing, you know exactly what is said in each response. You don't miss a word because you didn't hear it or it was mumbled. You can print out the conversation to use later. With e-mailing, the response may not be quite as quick, but it is in writing and you can print it out also. Many people prefer writing down their answers because it gives them time to think first, and they can include additional details they might not remember right away. If you and the person live in different time zones and you use e-mail, you don't need to worry about whether you are calling at a good time—not too early in the morning or too late at night.

Through a letter. It may seem old-fashioned to send a letter through the mail, but there are some people—especially the older generations—who truly prefer this method. You can handwrite or type your letter and, if you want to increase the chances of the

Getting a letter from overseas can be exciting.

person writing back, you can include an envelope with your name and address on it, plus a stamp. While this method may be slower—it can take three days for a letter to travel from one side of the country to the other (and up to several weeks if going internationally)—it can also be enjoyable.

Knowing What to Say

Conducting an interview may be as easy as sitting down to chat, but it takes preparation. No matter what kind of interview you choose to do, by doing some "interviewing homework" first, you will most likely get more information in less time.

Before the interview, sit down and make a list of the questions you want to ask. If you don't, you will probably find yourself with some uncomfortable silences and awkward pauses. Try to avoid any questions that can be answered with a simple yes or no. Instead, try asking open-ended questions that are best answered with an explanation. Can you see how these questions might inspire stories and memories? As you read the list, think about what other questions you might want to ask.

- Where did you live when you were a child? A house? An apartment? Can you describe it?
- Did you ever move? Where did you go, and how did you feel about it?
- Who were you named after? How do you feel about your name?
- What was your neighborhood like? Your city or town? Where did you like to go?
- What was your school like? Did you have a favorite teacher? What kind of student were you?
- What kind of clothing did you wear to school? What fads were in fashion at the time?
- Who was your best friend? What did you do together?
- What did your parents do as you were growing up?
- What was your first job? How did you feel about it? What did you do?

Was a paper route your dad's first job way back when?

- What hobbies did you have? What were some of your favorite games?
- Did you have pets? What kind? What were their names?
- Did you date? Whom did you date? What was a typical date like? How did you meet your spouse?
- Did you and your family have traditions for birthdays, holidays, etc.? How did they get started?
- What foods did your parents make? Which ones did you like best and least?
- When did you leave home? Why? How did it feel?
- What music was popular? Who were your favorite musicians?
- What historical events do you remember? Wars? Natural disasters? Economic hardships? Troubles in politics? How did these issues affect the family? What inventions do you especially remember?
- Did you go to college? If so, where? What did you study? What was it like there?

Maybe your dad was even in a rock group in high school. Ask him!

- Were you in the military? If so, which branch? What was it like? Did you fight in a war? Which one? Which battles were you in? What were your duties?
- Did you or your parents **emigrate** from another country? Which one? How old were you? What are your memories of this event?
- What was your wedding ceremony like? Who was there? Did you go on a honeymoon? Where to, and what was it like?

Although some people truly enjoy being asked a lot of questions like these, other relatives may not and may feel pressured to come up with a "right" answer. You can help those people by saying, "Tell me about your bedroom when you were little," or, "I'd love to hear about your neighborhood while you were growing up." By asking them to tell you about something, they may find it easier to talk and share their memories with you.

Tracing your ancestry begins with talking to the people you are related to—but it certainly doesn't stop there. Where else can you go for information and help? Let's find out.

If your family publishes a newsletter or web site for pre-reunion updates, you could put in an announcement about your project and ask relatives to come with stories, memories, and photos to share with you.

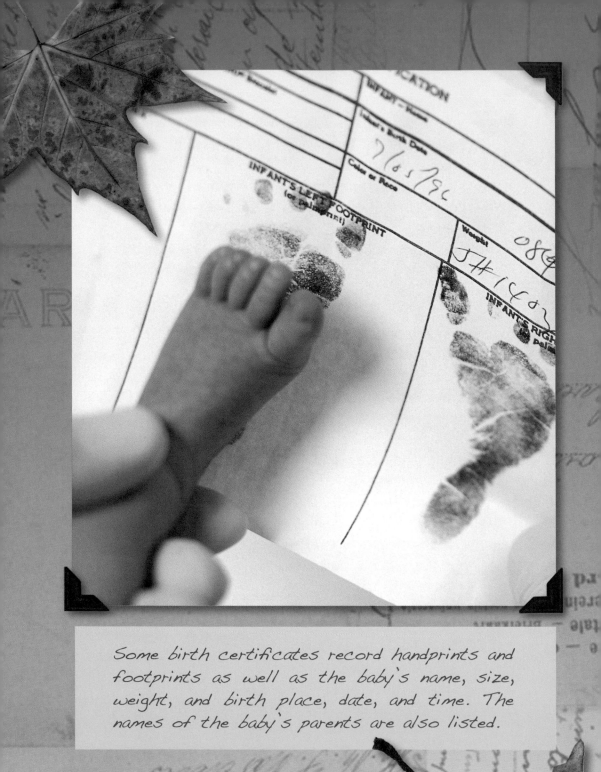

Some birth certificates record handprints and footprints as well as the baby's name, size, weight, and birth place, date, and time. The names of the baby's parents are also listed.

CHAPTER 4: GROWING A FAMILY TREE

Spending time getting stories and facts from your relatives is a great way to trace your family history back two, three, or even four generations. For many people, that is enough to create the family tree they had in mind. However, what if you would like to go back even farther? Perhaps you want to include those relatives who are no longer around. If you want to go back more generations, you will have to become an ancestor detective.

Reaching Out

Public records are just that—records that are open for the public to see. Because of the Freedom of Information Act of 1966, there are many types of documents from the U.S. government that can be accessed just by asking. Many of them contain important information about people. Some examples include:

- Birth certificates
- Death certificates
- Marriage certificates
- Military papers
- Church records
- Citizenship papers
- Passenger ship lists
- Census records

- Some school and college records
- Social Security records
- Some employment and occupational records
- Deeds and wills

To get these records, you can contact public offices such as courthouses, libraries, schools, cemeteries, and state archives. By writing or e-mailing these places, you'll know which places will be worth visiting in person. Check their web sites for important information such as whom to contact, address, and whether there are any charges involved (postage, copying, or other fees) for obtaining the information you want.

When writing a letter to any office or organization, remember to be two things: polite and precise. Make the person who is in charge of responding to your letter sigh in relief when they see a brief note that explains exactly what you are looking for—and asking nicely. Be sure to clearly state:

- What type of record you are interested in locating
- The full name of the person (including a maiden name if it is a married woman)
- Your relationship to the person whose records you are searching
- Any dates you already know or have confirmed

Before you send your letter, be sure to proofread it. When you write to a person or organization, take the time to correct any possible errors in spelling or grammar. Include any fees they may require (in a check or money order, not cash).

Page 33 shows an example of a letter asking for further information from either an organization or a genealogy group. The explanation for why you need to include each piece of material is in parentheses. When you send a letter, make sure to keep a copy

Your Name
Your Street Address
Your City, State, and Zip Code
Your E-mail Address

March 14, 20-- **(current date)**

Mr. John Miller **(specific person's name)**
Genealogy Queries Inc. **(name of group or organization)**
1111 Main St. **(street address)**
Washington, D.C. 20007 **(city, state and zip code)**

Dear Mr. Miller,
I am searching for the following information and am hoping that you can help me pinpoint it.

MORGAN. **(Person's surname in capitals for easy reference).** Madison Co., NY, USA **(county, state, and country you are interested in)** 1850–1900 **(years you are interested in finding out more about).** I'm searching for information about the children of Harrison MORGAN, who was born in 1802 in New York and died somewhere between 1875 and 1880. **(Statement of what you are searching for.)** His wife's name was Elaine and her maiden name was SCHWINDEL. They had at least six children but their names are not confirmed.

I have enclosed $4 for the cost of postage, per your web site's recommendation. Please feel free to e-mail me at [your e-mail address] if you have any questions. Thank you for your help. **(Always say "thank you" for the help they have given—or will give—you.)**

Sincerely,
(your signature)
Your Name

for yourself so that you can keep track of what you requested, from whom, and when. This is especially important if you are sending a number of letters.

Some genealogy buffs create their own forms called **correspondence** logs. Typically, these logs include columns for the day you sent the correspondence, the name and address of the person or organization, what information you asked for, when you received a reply, and what information you got. You can find blank correspondence logs on the Internet, or you can create your own. An accounting columnar pad can work well, or just a regular notebook from school. You can also create one on your computer using the "insert table" feature on word processing programs (such as Microsoft Word).

Organization is priceless when you are collecting a lot of information.

DATE	NAME/ADDRESS	REASON FOR LETTER	RESPONSE

You may be able to visit some of the places in person. For example, many original documents can be found in your state archives. They keep copies of military records, estate papers, county deeds, and land grants, as well as more personal documents such as diaries, letters, and photographs. To find your state archive, just go online. A list of each state's contact information can also be found at Ancestor Search: United States State Archive and Historical Society Addresses. You can often search through their inventory online, and order copies of documents, as well as find out where they are located in case you would like to go in person to take a look around.

Learning from the Documents

Once you have the documents that you requested or researched, what do you do with them? Start by reading these forms carefully for the details that you need. Find out exact dates, names, and locations. Remember that receiving one document will often lead to searching for another one. Genealogy is not a quick hobby with a clear-cut end. Instead, it tends to go on and on as you find out more and more. For example, if you find your great-great-grandfather's citizenship papers and they reveal that he came to the United States by ship, you can start searching for a passenger list or **manifest** with his name on it. A birth certificate can provide you

You might not have realized it, but many families begin with this exact moment!

with a baby's parents' names, which may lead to a marriage certificate.

Once you have gotten all the information you need from the document, be sure to file it away carefully in the notebook or files that you have created. Plastic page covers are excellent for holding and protecting documents and forms. You may need to refer to them later, so you'll want to keep them in good shape.

Looking into the past can be fascinating, especially when you can trace each step of people who lived a century or more ago right up to your own birth. Knowing where you came from is exciting, and searching for clues is a journey you will never forget.

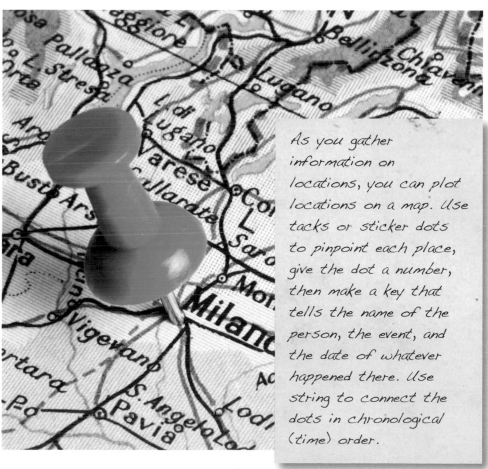

As you gather information on locations, you can plot locations on a map. Use tacks or sticker dots to pinpoint each place, give the dot a number, then make a key that tells the name of the person, the event, and the date of whatever happened there. Use string to connect the dots in chronological (time) order.

Imagine finding a photograph like this one. It shows the Eighth U.S. Army Air Force 352nd Fighter Group. How exciting it would be to find out you were related to someone in the unit.

CHAPTER 5:
SENDING OUT SHOOTS

There are many different types of documents and forms that can help you discover the past, but there are other ways to find important clues. Here are a few of them.

Capturing a Moment

A picture is supposedly worth a thousand words, and this is just as true in the field of genealogy. If you look carefully at old family photographs, you can learn a lot from their many clues.

When you first look at a picture, check the back to see if there is any writing. Sometimes it will list the names of the people in the photograph, as well as the date and location. If the photo is in an album, that information may be written underneath each picture.

What information can you find in a photo that isn't labeled? If there is a studio or photographer's name stamped on the photo, you can follow that clue. If the photo contains an image of a soldier or sailor, pay close attention to the uniform. With a magnifying glass, look closely at any medals or labels that could provide clues about rank and military branch. This information could guide you in a search of military records.

Look at the school desks, the girls' ribbons and braids, the policeman's uniform, and the girls' dresses. Using these clues might help you discover when the photograph was taken. A magnifying glass may help you find even more details.

Is the picture a school photo? Look for anything in the photo that indicates the name of the school. Look at the teacher, chalkboard, and walls for possible clues.

Examine the clothing and hairstyles in the photo. Those are clues to the time period in which they were taken. Accessories such as gloves, hats, and jewelry give additional information. In the background, cars, furniture, or other items such as telephones and television sets can help you figure out approximately when the photo was taken.

Look for family resemblances within the photos. Is there a nose that follows your family through each generation? A strong chin? Curly hair?

The type of photograph is also a clue to its age. The oldest type of photo is the **daguerreotype.** It was used from 1839 to

1860 and was made with silver-plated copper. The next photos were **tintypes,** made from iron, and **ambrotypes,** made from glass. They were used from 1850 to 1900. Next came **albumen prints**. These were printed on treated paper and were used from 1855 to 1910. These were followed by **platinum prints,** which had the first hints of color. Slides were popular from the 1940s to about the 1950s. Modern prints began in the 1950s. Of course, today, most photos are taken with digital cameras and stored electronically.

Spending Time in the Kitchen

One unexpected place that you might get some important clues to your family's ancestry is in your kitchen. Does your family have a recipe for a special dish that has been handed down through the generations? Perhaps Grandmother MaryAnn always makes oyster stew for Christmas, or birthdays are celebrated with a homemade peach pie instead of cake. Have you ever asked why? This is your chance!

If you are not sure whether your family has any of these recipe traditions, ask your siblings, parents, or grandparents. If there is such a dish, consider making it with a relative. As you cook or bake, ask questions about the recipe. Where did it get started? Who made it first? If it is a regional dish, did it come from a place your family used to live? What time of year was it usually served? Are there any special stories that go along with the dish? Take notes on what you find out. Create a form to chart the details, and include the name of the recipe or dish; who made it first and when; why it was first made; and what it celebrated.

Keeping Traditions

Another avenue to explore is your family's rituals or traditions. What do you do to celebrate special days or holidays that is unique to your family? Do you go to an unusual place, eat an unusual food, or give unusual gifts? Ask yourself why. If you do not know the answer, here is an opportunity to trace where those celebrations got started. You can use a form from the Internet (such as the one at *Family Tree Magazine*'s web site), or you can create your own. It should have spaces for a description of the tradition, including how it is carried out, from food served to clothing worn; when and where the tradition started, and by whom; who still practices the tradition; any documentation of it, such as photographs or diary entries; and extra notes, family comments, and research details.

Learning about Heirlooms

Have you ever noticed something in your house that your parents tell you came from their parents or grandparents? It might be a fancy dinner plate, a painting or statue, an old book, or an

A family heirloom can be as tiny but important to save as this pin, which took the place of an engagement ring for a grandfather (pictured in pin) and grandmother until they had enough money to buy real jewelry.

elaborate picture frame. Objects that are handed down from one generation to the next are called **heirlooms,** and the process of passing them is called **provenance.** These objects often have important ancestry stories behind them.

Ask your parents if they are aware of any such heirlooms in your family. If they know of one, try to find out the heirloom's history. Who first owned it, and how and when did the person obtain it? Who created it? How has the object been passed down? What stories go along with this item? Who owns the heirloom currently? Who will get it next? Keep track of this information in your notebook.

That old teapot your mom uses just might be an heirloom.

A Look Back in Time

Have you ever read a book about the past and realized how interesting history can be? Maybe you read about an amazing battle, a heroic figure, or even a cool invention. Finding out about the people and events that came before you can be fascinating. Also, knowing what happened in the past can make it easier to understand the present.

When you begin studying genealogy, you may experience the same thing. You are exploring how your family was created and who played roles in shaping it. Learning about who came before you can help you understand yourself better. By doing the research and becoming a detective, you can create your own family tree and place yourself right at the base. Good luck, and have fun!

BOOKS

Adolph, Anthony. *Who Am I? The Family Tree Explorer.* London: Quercus Books, 2009.

Beller, Susan Provost. *Roots for Kids: A Genealogy Guide for Young People.* Baltimore, MD: Genealogical Publishing Co., 2010.

Chang, Gilda. *Diversity Diaries: Kids Genealogy.* Bloomington, IN: AuthorHouse, 2006.

Ollhoff, Jim. *Beginning Genealogy.* Edina, MN: ABDO and Daughters, 2010.

Ollhoff, Jim. *Filling the Family Tree.* Edina, MN: ABDO and Daughters, 2010.

Wolfman, Ira. *Climbing Your Family Tree: Online and Offline Genealogy for Kids.* New York: Workman, 2010.

WORKS CONSULTED

This book is based on personal e-mail interviews with genealogist Juleigh Hobson on December 20, 2010, and on the following resources:

Archives.com: Search Family Trees and Vital Records
    http://www.archives.com/

Davis, Graeme. *Research Your Surname and Your Family Tree.* Oxford, UK: How to Books, 2010.

Family Tree.com
    http://www.familytree.com/

Galford, Ellen. *The Genealogy Handbook.* Pleasantville, NY: Readers Digest Publishing, 2001.

Hoole, Gavin, and Cheryl Smith. *The Really, Really, Really Easy Step-by-Step Guide to Creating Your Family Tree Using Your Computer: For Absolute Beginners of All Ages.* London, England: New Holland Books, 2009.

Mason, Jenn. *The Art of the Family Tree: Creative Family History Projects Using Paper Art, Fabric and Collage.* Minneapolis, MN: Quarry Books, 2007.

Powell, Kimberly. *The Everything Family Tree Book.* Avon, MA: Adams Media, 2006.

Worick, Jennifer. *Beyond the Family Tree: A 21st Century Guide to Exploring Your Roots and Creating Connections.* New York: Stewart, Tabori and Chang, 2010.

ON THE INTERNET

All Family Crests
http://www.allfamilycrests.com/

Ancestor Search: United States State Archive and Historical Society Addresses
http://www.searchforancestors.com/statearchives.html

Family Tree Kids!
http://kids.familytreemagazine.com/kids/welcome.asp

Family Tree Magazine: Free Forms
http://www.familytreemagazine.com/FREEFORMS

Free Family Tree Charts and Genealogy Forms
http://www.freefamilytreecharts.com/

Free Genealogy Charts & Forms—Family Tree Chart
http://genealogy.about.com/od/free_charts/ig/genealogy_charts/

Free Interactive Pedigree Chart
http://genealogy.about.com/od/free_charts/ig/genealogy_charts/pedigree_chart.htm

Genealogy for Kids
http://www.kidsturncentral.com/topics/hobbies/kidsgenealogy.htm

House of Names
http://www.houseofnames.com/

How to Design Your Own Family Crest
http://www.ehow.com/how_4855564_design-own-family-crest.html

Make Your Coat of Arms
http://www.makeyourcoatofarms.com/

Roots Web: Charts and Forms
http://helpdesk.rootsweb.com/get_started/charts_forms.html

Saskatchewan (Canada) Gen Web Project: Sask Gen Web for Kids
http://www.rootsweb.ancestry.com/~cansk/kids/sgwforkids.html

United States State Archive and Historical Society Addresses
http://www.searchforancestors.com/statearchives.html

World Famous Genealogy & Family Tree Charts
http://misbach.org/

WorldGenWeb For Kids
http://www.worldgenweb.org/~wgw4kids/

GLOSSARY

albumen print (al-BYOO-min PRINT)—An early photograph using paper covered in a solution of egg white and salt and dipped in silver nitrate.

ambrotype (AM-broh-typ)—An early photograph that used silver on glass.

correspondence (kor-eh-SPON-dunts)—Communication by letters, including e-mails, instant messaging, and other forms of writing between people.

crest (KREST)—A drawing or illustration that symbolizes a family or unit.

daguerreotype (duh-GAYR-oh-typ)—One of the first types of photographs, which created an image on a silver plate using iodine in the presence of mercury vapor.

emigrate (EH-mih-grayt)—To move out of one's home country.

genealogy (jee-nee-AH-luh-jee)—The study of one's ancestry.

heirloom (AYR-loom)—A valuable object that has belonged to a family for several generations.

interview (IN-ter-vyoo)—A meeting to find out information from a person.

maiden name (MAY-den NAYM)—A woman's surname before she marries.

manifest (MAH-nih-fest)—A document that lists the passengers and cargo on a ship.

maternal (muh-TUR-nul)—On the mother's side.

paternal (puh-TUR-nul)—On the father's side.

platinum print (PLAT-num PRINT)—A photograph that uses platinum salts rather than silver salts in the process.

provenance (PRAH-vuh-nunts)—The ownership history of an object such as an heirloom.

surname (SUR-naym)—A person's family name, which is often the last name.

tintype (TIN-typ)—Also called a ferrotype, an early photograph made on a thin, darkened piece of tin.

INDEX

archives   32, 35

birth certificates   18, 30, 31, 35, 37

Boy Scout Genealogy Merit Badge   7–8, 10

Carter, Ross   9

correspondence logs   34

family crest   19

family recipes   41

family reunions   23, 29

family traditions   41, 42–43

family tree charts   16–17

Freedom of Information Act   31

getting started   13–14

heirlooms   42–43

Hobson, Andrew   7–10

Hobson, Ian   8

interviews   19, 21–29

  computer   25

  conducting   26–29

  face-to-face   20, 22–23, 24–25

  letter   25–26

  questions to ask   26–29

  telephone   24–25

letters to public offices   32–34

manifests   35

maps   37

marriage certificates   31, 36, 37

Master Termite   7, 9–10

notebooks   11, 23, 34, 37, 41, 43

Parsons, John   8

pedigree charts   16

personal stories   4–5, 8–9, 13–14, 21, 27, 31

photographs   18, 22, 29, 35, 38, 39–41, 42

provenance   43

public records   30, 31–32, 35, 36, 37

puzzles   5, 10–11

resources   18–19

social networks   25

Those Devils in Baggy Pants   9

time frame   19, 40

Washington, Martha   4–5

weddings   18, 23, 29

ABOUT THE
AUTHOR

Tamra Orr is a full-time author living in the Pacific Northwest with her family. She has written more than 250 nonfiction books for readers of all ages. She has a degree in English and Secondary Education from Ball State University. Orr has been fascinated with her ancestry since the day she found out she is related to George Washington's wife. Since then she has constructed a number of family trees and is eager to add grandchildren to hers. In her fifteen minutes of free time, she loves reading, writing letters, and looking at Oregon scenery.